We Wh █████████ nons

Sober Sonnets

"I can imagine using Roger A.'s sonnets as discussion 'topics' at a
weekend retreat. That would be even better than reading them alone.
Actually, reading them in private was pretty great, too."

— Rockford, Illinois

"[Roger A.] really knows what goes on in my worst hours. Reading him
reinforced my determination and reminded me that the Higher Power has
a purpose for me today—for all the 'todays' to come.

— Milwaukee, Wisconsin

"I predict many, many more readers and groups will be as grateful as I
am that Roger A. has the courage to be so open in his journey. His record
of good days, bad days, pain and insight tells me there's more than hope
ahead, there [may be] beauty in the search."

— Indianapolis

We
Who
Battle
Demons

Sober Sonnets

Roger A.

afterword by Huey C.

Parkhurst Brothers, Inc., Publishers
Little Rock, Arkansas

Parkhurst Brothers books are distributed to the trade through the Chicago Distribution Center, a unit of the University of Chicago Press, and may be ordered through Ingram Book Company, Baker & Taylor, Follett Library Resources and other book industry wholesalers. To order from the University of Chicago's Chicago Distribution Center, phone 1-800-621-2736 or send a fax to 800-621-8476. Copies of this and other Parkhurst Brothers Inc., Publishers titles are available to organizations and corporations for purchase in quantity by contacting Special Sales Department at our home office location, listed on our web site.

Printed in Canada

First Edition, February, 2011 (Pre-publication copies distributed in late 2010 fall under the same copyright]

2011 2012 2013 2014 2015 2016 2017

17   16 15 14 13 12 11 10 9 8 7 6 5 4 3 2 1

Library of Congress Control Number:
Please consult our website, www.pbros.net and look for the section for librarians.

ISBN: Trade Paperback: 978-1-935166-42-9
Ten- digit: 1-935166-42-5

ISBN: e-book: 978-1-935166-43-6
Ten-digit: 1-935166-43-3

Book designer and/ cover designer: Harvill Ross Studios Ltd.

Acquired for Parkhurst Brothers Inc. by: Ted Parkhurst

For Craig, Chris, Bud, David, Jerry,
Marcia, Sara, Kevin, and Charlie

These poems, with all their crudities, doubts, and confusions,
are written for the love of Man and in praise of God,
and I'd be a damn fool if they weren't.
— Dylan Thomas

Table of Contents

HOW SHE DANCED

My sister Joan died today. Heart attack
shut down the brain, so her children turned off
the respirator. Truth is, she pushed back
from life years before, kidnapped by Smirnoff
or such poison, victim of that disease
that stalks me daily, wants me to explode
and take folks with me, sends me to my knees
praying for help. When we were young, she told
me she'd be a star. A true beauty, she
burned inside for fame and romance, could bend
crowds with wit, charm, and, oh, how she danced: free
and graceful, flowing across stage like wind
through prairie grass. Married twice. Bore a girl
and two boys who loved her. For all the world.

DISTURBED CHARACTER

What's wrong with me? I keep making the same
mistakes, hurling my will at loved ones and
others through psychic lethal weapons: flames
of fear, javelins of jealousy, canned
sarcasm, rocks of rage. Then apologize,
offer lilies of lies, illusive tears.
Stand stunned or slump insulted when chastised,
rebuked. I can never trust what appears
as truth from others' mouths. They say my crimes
include never seeing consequences.
What's that supposed to mean? Can't they tell I'm
special, a great mind trying to make sense
of life? How, though I'm a step above them,
I struggle to understand and love them?

ROGUE WAVES

Sometimes rippling of our bodies beyond
small obstacles and openings diffracts
into impotent night. Sometimes second
thoughts form rage-forced currents, brutal, exact
as surgeons' knives dissecting our senses,
our vital organs, memory and hope.
Sometimes during parties, my flesh winces
as I slouch on thick couch, smoking bad dope,
a coastal island enveloped by sea
of pillows, you lying on flushed carpet
with spilled drink, our outbursts storming sadly
through old friends, sweeping them past parapets
of tolerance. Wounded dolphins, they dive
in swift retreat, desperate to survive.

WEATHER VAIN

Cloudy morning. Cloudy memory. What
did she murmur before she left? Something
about drowning. Yeah. Being bound to slats
of our bed and drowning in the storm. Sting
of my glare, she said. *I know all about
drowning*, I said. Then she closed the door. *I
know my fear scars you,* I wanted to shout.
*I know my binges drag you under. Why
can't I stop? Listen, I promise you. This
time I'll pour it out and toss the bottle.
This time I'll show up for dinner. I'll kiss
you, hand you flowers. Care for your brittle
heart instead of sneaking away to play
around* . . . Yeah. I'd have said that, if she'd stayed.

STORM

drifting this way through night like wool blanket
over sweaty torso, dragging its slow
thick weight off soaked bed. Heat lightning flanks it
like dire, dying neon sign. Slight wind blows
warnings of coming gusts, then steady sweep
of howls, pellets splattering our shaky
panes. Now something like a storm sharply leaps
through me, starting to lash like harsh waves we
swam drunk on nights when rash squalls assaulted
us. Remember Lake Ouachita that dark
July when we challenged its width, vaulted
dead branches and dove deep, then rose to stark
chill of reality, both breast-stroking
back to near shore, slurring in our joking?

ENDGAME

I keep hearing this muffled voice. Can't sleep
for a week. Coming through thin bedroom walls,
this thing like a kidnapper's phone threat, creep
snarling haunting notes—digital owl's call
hooted through a spy's keychain voice changer:
You . . . you in your sin and shame . . . must face your
endgame . . . Some nights it sounds like a stranger,
cantor of bitter loss. Some nights I'm sure
it's her, sneaking to disguise her bitch howl.
Last night I lost it. Nearly shot my fist
through my neighbor's wall. Slipped out in a cowl,
prowling streets, feeling devils slash my wrists
with talons. Gallons of booze I've swallowed
can't deaden this sense I'm being followed.

SONG: KILL MYSELF ALL OVER AGAIN

I kill myself all over again
kill myself all over again

Intoxication
much like taxation
and masturbation
just brings frustration
still I kill myself all over again
kill myself all over again

I'm goin' out tonight
my body's all uptight
filled with electric fright
I wanna have some fun
I plan to just drink **one**
now the marathon's begun
and I kill myself all over again
kill myself all over again

Jill says she's gonna
smoke marijuana
Bill says he'll join her
for marijuana
I don't wanna
smoke marijuana
still I kill myself all over again
kill myself all over again

I stagger way out back
to find my old friend Jack
in a doorway smokin' crack
I slur *Gimme that crack*
and I kill myself all over again
kill myself all over again

In trips our buddy Beth
We snort her crystal meth
I shake and fight for breath
while we laugh and scream of death
and I kill myself all over again
kill myself all over again

Now I'm really whacked
so it's fine when I hear Jack
wheeze *I got a bag of smack*
so we stumble to his shack
and I kill myself all over again
kill myself all over again

Intoxication
much like taxation
and masturbation
just brings frustration
and I kill myself all over again
kill myself all over again
kill myself all o . . .
kill myself a . . .
kill m . . .
ki . . .

AUTO MOTIVES AND LOCO MOTIVES

The former carry me slyly up your
driveway at night. I circle past lighted
windows, slow as a tear trail, stay alert
for any movement inside. Once sighted,
I stomp the pedal, shatter through locked doors,
crashing into your living room or den.
The latter hurtle over countrysides
of fleeing bodies, bolting me through glens
of former peace where now chaos presides,
condemning every witness, crushing poor
souls who dash to stay on track, yet tumble
under my raging wheels. Call it impulse.
Cite incentive. You won't hear me grumble.
My guzzling molds goads my mind can't repulse.

LAST NIGHT

And now honeysuckle's aroma, thick
as syrup, fills my nostrils like the breath
of my old lover on that night her slick
frame poured over me, just before her death,
her bourbon-coated whisper pleading first
for pain, then caress, then pain again, as
if she hoped for all before the end. Nursed
too long by my soft words, she cursed our last
lovemaking, the honeysuckle bouquet
I had brought to make peace. Neither of us
knew. Drunk, angry, again I lost my way:
A right sent her off the bed; her head just
missed the wrought-iron chair. She dressed, slammed the door.
The cop's call left me crying on the floor.

SPONSOR

When you called phenomenon of craving
an allergy, the Rubik's cube clicked in
place—how drink's comfort followed with raving
night after night, waking next day in den
of pain, razor blades of fear and despair
slashing every pore, finding brief relief
only through drink again, hoping to pare
the party down to just one beer, belief
my brain could control my hand's insane grasp
for the glass, suffering once more my soul
soar then slowly crush into dust. When you clasped
my hand, your clear eyes glowing as Rigel
and Sirius gleam, at once I sensed our
first step in seeking some higher power.

Al tells Bill, "I'm powerless." Bill tells Chad,
"I'm crazy." Chad tells Don, "I let go and
let God." Don tells Edward, "I soul search." Ed
tells Ferdinand, "I confess." Ferdinand
tells George, "I'm ready." George tells Henry, "I'm
released." Henry tells Ira, "I review."
Ira tells Jack, "I amend." Jack tells Kim,
"I take stock." Kim tells Len, "I continue
contemplation." Len tells me, "I try to
carry on." I tell Al, "I'm powerless."
That's how it goes with our small retinue.
Then we scatter, remember how we're blessed.
Pay attention as we move and speak. Hope,
if asked, we can help a sufferer cope.

PRAYER

Great Breather, reach down from your pinnacle,
blessing all you touch or pass in reaching,
and reach me, grasping with your tentacle,
claw, hand, hoof, or paw, and without preaching
simply lift me from this cave of howling
wind—its cold, dark walls hemming my body
and psyche in crushing shame, my scowling
heart palpitating *no hope no shoddy*
hope no hope—your merciful grip casting
out pain and memory, deeming only
instant knowing, feeling everlasting
warmth of your eyelight, no longer lonely,
no longer gashed by spirit's whiplash (cost
of gnashing fear), no longer lost soul lost.

ARMAGEDDON

We don't have much time, so listen. I've tried
for years to crawl into hell, shoving souls
who're in my way. Probably should have died
at least five times. Fought reason to control
fate—maniacal drunk battling bouncers
at closing time. It's not some unholy
trinity who strips you of grace, pounds your
face into concrete, rolls your limp body
down jagged crevices of despair, cures
your rebellion with steel-toed kicks in groin
and gut. It's those confused, loving eyes, pure
and simple, gazing down at you like coins
melting in flame, silent deafening pleas
begging you to let go, set the beast free.

WHAT COLOR'S THE SKY?

Over salads at the outdoor cafe,
her autumn hair glowing like her cream skin,
watching a soaring bluebird make its way,
she recalled being too drunk for driving
to JFK. So she hired a limo
to pick up her boyfriend, back from LA
and a spot shoot. Deep shame flaming primo
in her heart flared to anger, then display
of curse words spewing, shocking her smiling
beau as he slid in the back seat. His face
burned to ash, eyes of tears, voice compiling
one soft phrase: *What color's the sky?* Disgraced,
stunned, she blurted . . . *Blue* . . . He whispered, *Bluer . . .
hell of a lot bluer . . . when you're sober.*

REFLECTION

Broadway and Bleecker. Northeast corner. Noon.
Weekday. Striding to a meeting, I pause
in summer heat. Gaze at my reflection
in McEerie's window. I hear applause
in my head, shouts of how I'm looking good.
Suddenly my image darkens. My eyes
stare past me to the bar. He's drooling food,
greasy semi-liquid swarming like flies
on his worn, gray Jimi Hendrix sweatshirt,
dead guitarist's red-ink profile fading
to pink. The guy gawks toward me, face absurd
parched clay, eyes lost in flashing, cascading
electroshock. He guzzles down a beer.
It's '91. A year ago, I'm there.

DERACINATION

By '79, parched from booze and scum
spirit—my shrunken psyche torn away,
lost to any tender, structured stratum
called home—I tumbled northeast. Frigid spray,
incessant wind of iced Atlantic tossed
me across Jersey Shore's edge, up mired coast
to Greenwich Village, nearly brain-dead, lost
as mite in beehive, gnarled meristem frost-
bitten, sapped of will, then strangely anchored
in church basements, libraries, museums,
soft, sober voices replacing rancor,
invisible power—psychic phloem—
nurturing all, my creative rebirth
lifting me back to native Southern earth.

DARKENED WINDOW

Once, in Greenwich Village, 5 or after,
Saturday fall sun flickering behind
those short roofs west on Houston, their laughter—
those silhouetted ladies' charm—windchimed
out that narrow bar door. They claimed my glance
through darkened window, first sight mirrored glow
filtering through liquor bottles. *Let's dance!*
one smokescarred soprano cawed out. I bowed
my head, wishing she were summoning me,
then shrugged in shame having wished it, knowing
I really craved the old routine: whiskey
sip flowing to lust to maybe crowing
naked at dawn, or drubbed by some bouncer.
I grabbed my cell phone and called my sponsor.

CABLES

My thoughts shuffle how I feel. My feelings
mangle efforts to think. So I get mixed
up, like briars. Must resort to kneeling
in prayer, confess all, admit I can't fix
myself. Listen. Sense my tangled cables
unfold like thick roots reaching for water,
thin branches stretching to sunlight, able
to focus a moment, then another.
Something glows deep within these vibrating
wires, but I can't make it out. Must I track
you down again? How I keep debating
forgotten propositions, leading back
to my mute, multi-angled starting line,
reseeking lost cables to the divine.

THE POWER OF KEEPING IT SIMPLE

I'm not drinking today. I don't know why,
really, except someone said to come here
every day. And someone said take this book
and read it, and then let's talk. And someone
said I just couldn't stop, and my life went
to hell, nearly killed my wife one night when
she grabbed my Wild Turkey and threw it out.
And someone said me too. And someone said
I just drank beer, never took any drugs.
And I said me too. And someone said you
need to tell her you were wrong. And I said
can't I just tell you. And someone just looked
at me and didn't speak until I said
I'll go tell her now. And someone said on
your way, stay quiet and pray. And as I
was leaving the room, someone said my first
name, shook hands, and then said keep coming back.
I do that. And I'm not drinking today.

POLAR BEARS

Author on "Book TV" relates how male
polar bears avoid monogamy, eat
females and cubs when unearthing their trails.
Sounds like active alcoholics, replete
with ego-centered fear, caring only
to quench endless craving, devouring flesh
of any who fall in their sight, lonely
in constantly stalking vast tundra, fresh
blood turned to lip scabs, mushy snow melting
to muddy wasteland beneath their paws. I'll
tell you this, buddy: When I drank, pelting
hail and flooding streets couldn't stop me while
I struggled to reach a bar. Step in my
way, I'd scream and punch you . . . or slump and cry.

QUESTIONS

How do I not drink on a night like this
when news has shattered my heart? How do I
not lock my door and taste poison's last kiss
from some glass's moist lip when my body's
memory lurches, suddenly startled
awake, craving surging through every pore?
What process of blind faith has even led
me to ask you this? Who will dare keep score
once I start my fatal marathon? Why
should I even care? My dark soul falls lost,
doesn't it, hopeless in alcohol's wry
abyss, twisting through endless void? What cost
to you if I grow numb? (What power's there
still, leading me to kneel, whisper a prayer?)

I form vowels and consonants, calling
you Great Breather, calling on you always
to take from me or give me or please bring
me or deliver me and rarely praise
and thank you for breath and heartbeat, for brain
waves and enzymes, for senses and psyche,
for air, water, fire, and earth, for great pain
that always leads me back to honesty,
facing my power void, my reliance
on whispering fragments of your ancient
name. Every syllable within my chants
is you, every sound I confess, relent,
rely on to form bonds with your great soul
forming our souls, fragments of you, yet whole.

THE FERMENT I GROW FROM

Soil and slough pool where spirit draws its long
deep breath and our cell splits to two cells, this
exploding first encounter with passion
evolving to us in art's catharsis
this very moment. Once I realize
it all relates, I'm forever sharing,
arousing the universe itself. Eyes
cannot ignore energy's great daring
feat in every intelligent ounce of earth.
Years ago, riding home from Manhattan
to the Jersey Shore, questioning all worth
in life, through my bus window I caught glance
of a creek's swirling water: lithe dancer
recalling all birth. I'd found my answer.

SUICIDE WATCH

It's one of those days. Walking through Greenwich
Village, I must stop every block, check store
windows for my reflection, feel slight twitch
in my cheek, heartbeat's pace, deep breathe before
I realize I'm still here. Old demons
have sneaked back in, whisper need for relief,
recall favorite bars' sweet lights and fun,
ignore past patterns as liar and thief
who'll crush friends' and lovers' hearts for drink's sake.
I watch my face in McEerie's pane glass,
hear some nice guy within me: *A mistake
to go in there. Death knell. This too shall pass.*
I move away. Yet a voice like Barney
the barkeep keeps calling, *What'll it be?*

SILENCE

Like Preault's *Le Silence*, I place finger
to lips. Not to quiet you, love, but let
you know I'm tired of our quarrel, linger
in shadows to hear you rant. You forget
how, when I drank, my rage sent you hiding,
made you wonder if you'd survive the night.
Now you suffer your first dry days, fighting
it all the way, vowing you'll never sight
a meeting, will conquer your beast on your
own, not follow me just to please me, not
let me control your life, not play some pure
virgin to seduce. Accuse me of plots
to get you sober. I'm mute as a monk,
since I carry the message, not the drunk.

THOSE WHO THIRST

I feel them because I share their terror
on nights I resist or forget to pray,
so filled with my old addiction's tremor,
prelude to my body's earthquake, display
for seismic measure of my soul. It's not
always violent vibration. Often
it lays in wait, subtle as a despot
ready to behead a faithless mate. Then
there's simply some TV ad, creeping down
to my tongue from eyes captured by teardrops
of Budweiser cascading from moist brown
bottle after the pour. It sent Cyclops
to the floor. Yeah, that was wine, but poison's
poison. Will I heed my sponsor's lesson?

WE WHO BATTLE DEMONS

usually lose. Refuse to listen
to inner music, spirit song. Drown out
pulse with booze and excuses, determined
to win by retreat, shield off faith with doubt.
Yet a few of us, breathless, beaten, may
pause, sense some faint melody inviting
within, drop our weapons, and softly say
to ourselves, not even understanding
why, *Time to dance*. Slowly, slowly we start
to sway, feeling our center bring balance,
body's rhythm aligned with beating heart,
finding hope not through fighting but the dance.
We look for demons. They've vanished, inept
in facing our yielding to graceful steps.

WHISKEY BOTTLE FULL OF WORMS

I thought Lowell had called how I'd end up.
No cremation ashes. No sealed casket
to trap me, metal cocoon. Let grubs sup
on my skull and spleen from a mesh basket
buried in Mets' centerfield. Put in my
will to dig it up when they win a World
Series again. Scoop vermes in used rye
bottles, Old Overholt maybe, then furled
in some bloody towel from my last bar
fight. Hang it high on that rusted flag pole
over McEerie's. Hope old buddies far
and wide would cheer me once a year. My soul's
home didn't matter. It does now. I pray
instead of drink. Give thanks for sober days.
Ask not to resent Delgado's high pay.

plants one boot on the rail, eyes the barkeep
and says, "Bartender, give me a shot of
Jack Daniels." Barkeep goes over and sweeps
a full jigger in front of him. Guy shoves
the shot glass away to the right without
even taking a sip. He says, "Now pour
me another one." Guy takes it, then shouts,
and gulps down the whiskey. He slugs a score
down just that way, twenty empty glasses
lined up along the bar. Before he serves
him again, barkeep says, "Someone passes
his first shot glass up. Why is that?" Guy swerves,
burps, slurs (clearly gone the way of the skunk),
"My sponshur shays da firsht drink gets ya drunk."

plants its hoof on the rail, eyes the barkeep
and says, "Give me a beer, will ya." Shakes its
mane. Barkeep blinks, but knows he's not asleep.
Shakes his head. Asks, "You want a schooner, Schlitz
or what?" "How about a Guinness," the horse
suggests. *Must be a Lougherne stud*, ponders
the keep. *Still he's only a horse. Of course*
he don't know nothin' of money. Wonder
if he even has any. Grabs a stout
and slides it down to the stud who guzzles
it, whinnies, then pulls some dollar bills out.
"Fifty bucks!" spouts the keep. The horse nuzzles
out fifty. "Don't get many horses here,"
quips the keep. Horse walks away with a leer:
"No wonder, charging fifty bucks a beer."

RESURRECTION

Deep in our roots far from light, something stirs:
desires to stop drinking. Nutrient's slow
surge consumes trunk, our course bark, even spurs
willowed branches to rise, spread wide, and now
withered leaves, charred black with wrinkled deadness,
seem to shudder, flex, grow green from within,
veins alive and sensing sun, limitless
air, letting wind caress each leaf's brief skin,
lift it in waving prayer and graceful dance.
At night, high leaves face stars. Our lean, long arms
open to moonlight and all it brings. Chance
becomes a sacred thing. Fearless of harm
from disease or storms, we stand still, aware
of where and who we are, Great Breather's care.

VALENTINE CARD WALKS INTO A BAR

Stands about six feet tall, with two red hearts
on its cover, each with eyes and a mouth.
They speak in unison, giving a start
to the barkeep. "An oat beer for our drouth,
good sir." He serves up two steins of maple
oat ale. They swill the drafts and call for more.
After two new rounds of spirit staples,
both hearts begin to sing: *Heart and Soul, Poor
Heart*, then *You Gotta Have Heart*. One problem:
They try harmony, but just can't carry
a tune. Angry customers shout at them.
"Quiet!" yells the barkeep, gravely harried.
"You're flagged! Ugh! How can you sing as bad as that?"
"Greeting cards," they reply, "are made to be flat!"

FORGETTING WHO YOU ARE

I get lost sometimes, can't conceive what's real.
I don't mean drinking, but stumbling sober
through normal days. As if ghostly thieves steal
my senses, roll my numb carcass over
a cliff onto a street where humans walk
around me, like I'm a fallen phone pole.
At meetings, I slouch and refuse to talk
but flare inside, afraid to say who stole
my identity. A girl's smile, a guy's
two-word critique. That's all it takes to make
my body earthquake within. No reply
though, just deeper retreat. Later, I fake
interest in talk over dinner, swear
to my sponsor I'm fine. He knows better.

BURNING STREETLAMP IN THE DARK

You want rigorous honesty? I feel
like a burning streetlamp in the dark, wrapped
in black glass so I can never reveal
my glowing light, my flaming psyche trapped
in unseen capsule hanging overhead.
Your heart ever felt enwrapped in barbed wire,
fiber gouged and slashed each beat, so you've bled
to death inside, gut a raging bonfire
consuming air meant for your lungs? You know
why I've called. You've flared this way or something
close. You let me spew out my pain. Words flow
like lava, but you don't run. I'm meaning
to stay alive. Keep faith. Not say screw it.
Most of all not drink. Pray I walk through it.

ONCE MORE, THEY'RE STILL

Again, Great Breather, you've silenced morbid
quarrels in my mind, quelling my brutal
committee's condemnations, laid torpid
those bitter, slashing tongues despising all
I am. Slugging shots and popping pills may
numb harsh slurs for a moment. Hazy smoke
can glaze their eyes and make them dumb for, say,
half a day. Yet soon I wake to brash pokes
from their scepters, lie shaking, awaiting
earthquakes of their lies. Then feel my lost soul
scream above them, sense despair abating
through my simple prayer: *Help . . . me.* They cajole
me, changing tactics. Then their spotlights fade.
I meditate within your peaceful shade.

BEFORE YOU PUT THE BOTTLE

or gun to your mouth, give me a call. I'll
tell how I obsessed over suicide
at seven years sober, raw flesh numb while
each shaking breath reeked with methyl bromide,
every swallow jagged shards of shattered
mirrors through my chest and gut. She had gone,
money dissolved, ego a smashed platter,
my higher power tossed a bitter bone
and shoved in a dungeon. Or so I thought.
How did I know you can't imprison love?
It kept shoving me to meetings, then taught
me to pay attention. I sensed safe coves
when I heard a guy say: *Get honest. Pray.*
Help someone. I work on these every day.

EUGENE O'NEILL

He wrote and drank and drank and wrote and drank.
He suffered from depression. Before all
this, he drank himself into the sick tank
for tuberculosis. I guess you'd call
his stay a spiritual experience:
there he first pledged himself to playwriting.
He won Pulitzers, the Nobel. You'll wince
to hear he disowned his daughter, felt sting
of two sons' suicides. Of course, divorced
a couple of times. Man, it makes me sad
they never lived that wilderness, his source
for youthful fantasy. Tremors so bad,
his last decade of life he couldn't write.
That moon made me think about him tonight.

In Manhattan, for a few years I worked
near Times Square. Would often cross 43rd
Street and Broadway. Finally saw the plaque
nailed to southeast corner building's absurd
pillar, giving it purpose: It marks his
birthplace, once a hotel, now a Starbucks.
Reads, "America's greatest playwright." This
still rings true. Hundreds of walkers, cars, trucks,
buses pass that plaque each day, not knowing
it's there. But I do. And now you do. So
if your personal equation's going
to NYC, pay homage. Whisper low,
"Man is born broken. He lives by mending.
The grace of God is glue." Angels will sing.

ALWAYS AN ALLMAN FAN

When Duane's motorcycle hit the flatbed
in '71, soon after *Fillmore*
East went gold, then their bassist Berry's head
crushed in another cycle crash, the four
survivors voted to carry on. How
can you not become a fan of courage
drowned in pain? How can you not pray for raw
talent, witnessing their suffering scourge
of turmoil, drugs, separation, lives so
similar to our own? Here's irony
of it all, love: how artists bow and go
forward to meet the Muse with spirits free
yet driven there by everlasting fire.
How do we separate grace from desire?

YOU, MY POWER

I touch my right thumb to index finger,
consider my cells and nerves, how I used
booze as anesthetic, never lingered
long where touch would incite caring, abused
senses and psyches, my own and others,
blind to mirror's reflection, deaf to words
of lovers, sixth sense inept to bother
about weddings and funerals, absurd
in my terrified mind. But now, drinking
soda without Cutty Sark, water sans
wine at dinner, my clear brain now linking
a spree with that first sip, I can make plans
for soft nights of honest love, follow through
caressing hands and lips, all prayers to You.

CRAVING THE ENEMY

Enough of this fearful plodding to find
serenity. I want to change the way
I feel. My body's nest of wasps, my mind
a sandstorm blinding vision, sweep away
all reason not to drink. I want to change
the way I feel. Cover my flesh, stripped and
raw as a martyr's corpse, with ancient, strange
aphrodisiacs. Wrap my brain in bands
of thick liqueurs, sweet as a prostitute's
pores. Drown out my soul's poor reality
with rich shots of Daniels or Dickel. Shoot
me. Stab me. Anything to set me free
from having to own myself, my demons,
forced to face life as an honest human.

LIGHT FADING TO NOTHING

I slouched blinded to taking the first step.
Slinked into rooms to get a woman back.
Couldn't envision life without drink. Kept
silent in last rows, huddled like a sack
of empty beer cans, wracked bones crinkling when
I'd flinch at an offered hand, wary of
eyes like Christmas candles, suspicious grins,
voices chiming bullshit like *let us love*
you till you can love yourself. I didn't
stay long. A few miserable months. Slipped
on slick peel of fear, slid on old resent-
ments back to my neighborhood sports bar. Whipped
down six quick O'Doul's, kidding myself. Then
came Coors, Black Jack. Of course, blacked out again,
tumbling inside craving's endless turbine.

SURRENDERING TO CLARITY

I lied my way to insanity, turned
silver chains of care into barbed wire for
ripping loved ones' flesh and psyches, then burned
old photos of family just to soar
alone through paranoia's black-ink mist.
Denial portrayed falling as flying.
Shocked by my drunk frame's crashing, I'd insist
I was fit to fly again; thought lying
paralyzed in my disease's mire would
appear to others a heavenly state.
But now this sponsor guy tells me I should
surrender every day. Man, how I hate
being told what to do. Still, my hazy
brain believes him when he says I'm crazy.

DEFINING MOMENT

I struggled for some image of higher
power; finally returned to Webster's.
God [note capital G]: *the supreme or*
ultimate reality. A lantern's
glow. *Reality.* That's what my soul fled
for thirty years through drinking—a downhill
run, then plunge, then starkest bottom. I read
more, sensing dominion, great yet gentle.
god [note small g]: *any person or thing*
deemed worthy of worship. I huffed a laugh.
Whispered how that capsules my troubles, stings
of who I really am. Folding in half
the magic page, closing the book, I stayed
quiet a while, then closed my eyes and prayed.

FOURTH STEP

I ran from it, frightened of revealing
my sick secrets. Morning before my fourth
anniversary, I sealed it, kneeling
in thanks, calling my sponsor, smiling mouth
asking for help on the fifth. He okayed
the next week. That night I wanted to drink,
body's old reflexes flinching from days
when celebration simply meant no-think
guzzling to senseless sleep. I slogged through three
meetings, obsession at last lifting when
I admitted my craving. Heads agreed
with my longing, nodding yes to my yen
for lie's soaring, recalling their own sad
yearnings to breathe false balm of Gilead.

THE NIGHT MY DAD DIED

in Yuba City, CA, worn away
by life, I was drunk on the Jersey Shore,
no good to him or my brother. I'd flay
selfish lines when I got the call, then swore
when I hung up, pissed to learn I'd grub no
insurance money for booze. Farted off
the funeral. Sober a while now, so
ashamed I keep making amends, I scoff
no more at words like "faith," "spirit," "moral."
Years later, sat with my brother by our
mom's deathbed, humble effort to ease soul's
journey. Stayed through that soft, sad final hour.
"Don't plan on how you'll feel," my sponsor would say.
"Just feel." I did that. She died on my birthday.

TRUTH WITHIN A SOFT FLAME

Pulling out my fourth step's typed pages, I
began to rattle off old transgressions.
My sponsor quickly stopped me, saying, "Why
don't I light a candle? For confession,
let's invite God in." He lit the candle.
It's soft flame calmed my heart. My voice assumed
an easy cadence. What seemed dire scandals
turned to faded ghosts. At times I presumed
my action irredeemable, this world's
lone scar. He'd nod. Say, "I did the same thing."
Finding him human, my surprised brain swirled
briefly. Then sensed relief. Our hours talking
led to silence. I said, "Done." He said, "Good."
We went out for food. Spoke of gratitude.

ASHES SOAR HIGH

So now I'm complete to this textured point,
soul's cavity scraped of sinful decay,
crushed offenses laid in a row, conjoined
in patterns revealing my defects. Say
I'm a new man. You'd cite feeling not fact.
We've neared a great first half. Now to spend time
alone, reflect, invite conscious contact,
measure my willingness to replace crimes
with actions of honest service, let go
of all to the Great All. Time to light my
own candle. Time to bind and place ego
over the flame, let its ashes soar high
as sacrifice: prayer to hold hands steady
as sign my entire being is ready.

HOW MASKS STAY SEALED

I've learned, at last, *humble* derives from Greek
meaning *earth*. As basic as life gets. I've
learned *humility*, for me, means to seek
reality, become aware I thrive
in its power, accept how masks stay sealed
to my face until this one higher source
chooses to remove them. When it's revealed
me to myself, I pray, *Keep me on course
through this day and night. Sober actions, please.*
Then I try to pay attention to all
I think, feel, and say; do I move with ease
through gifted air as honest soul, or fall
back on fear, try to suck another's breath
away, assuring relationship's death.

SOON I'LL APPROACH THEM

This infernal list I dreaded so long,
this internal death row of shame at last
scratched on paper, putting names to past wrongs,
those loved ones and others—honesty casts
me no longer as victim. Preps my heart
to open like small glass case of humble
pebbles at wounded royalty's ramparts.
This concrete row of humans I've stumbled
through, shoving them aside with vile ego,
doesn't even conceive it awaits me.
Soon I'll approach them, softly let them know
I wish to come talk, write how I'm sorry
if they're far off, or call them, it depends.
State clearly my intent to make amends.

TO LOVE AS NEVER BEFORE

I reviewed exact words with my sponsor,
then went and knocked on her door. Told her how,
sober, I pictured her nights of terror—
not knowing what monster lurked, form embowed
like a hunchback, soon to rage through our rooms,
an insane storm. Explained I no longer
explode as beast, now work for peace, assume
roles of quiet service, thanks to stronger
spirit deep within, gift of our breathing
universe. She took it better than I'd
hoped. (Not everyone has.) On my leaving,
I'd descend steps of her new home, sad pride's
crust of crushed dust stuffed in my pocket. Say
to myself, *This* is *the easier way.*

QUARRELS IN THE TUNNEL

I lie when I'm afraid. Often like some
TV voice promoting a weedeater,
sounding sharp while inside psyche succumbs
to dis-ease, reminds me how I teeter
toward a drink in subtle ways. Rarely now
I'll connive like a killer, bury grace
in my backyard garden, hoping somehow
to cover up truth with a smiling face,
knowing this new relationship soon will lay
alongside her. I've learned now how to stop, change
course, what simple steps to take and allay
quarrels in the tunnel, capping this strange
desire to self-destruct, stop feeling. Only
my actions say if I'm happy or lonely.

For years, like a snake, I sneaked through women's
bodies' dark lanes, hid there, couldn't conceive
them as human beings. Then would rage when
they'd stumble away crying, call me thief,
slam doors in my face, on my knuckles or
foot, scratch my name from private diaries
and emails. I tried poems and flowers
but colors couldn't camouflage my lies.
Then one day I tossed the booze. Not alone.
Learned from others through meetings and action.
Found how honesty cements fragile bones
of a sober day. Still, I find friction
burns when touching women. My shrink contends
we try to become lovers before friends.
At least I see how to make true amends.

I STARE INSIDE

I see a distant flash of light and think
about her eyes, blue aurora at night,
feel flaming wind within me. Should I drink
to intensify this moment or fight
its mystifying flight? What's my excuse
to break open a case of chaos one
more time? Is it my will calling abuse
a lover, or ancient craving alone
pushing me from my cell phone, stumbling toward
that fateful glass? I perceive some power
rushing me to my knees, fantasize swords
gashing my bowed head, sense bloody shower
across my carcass and carpet. I stare
inside flinching closed lids, whisper a prayer.

IT IS YOU

I pay attention to my slow breathing,
realize all life's a gift. My fingers
touch my daughter's sculpture, angels wreathing
throughout my bright living room. One lingers
by her homage to meditation: calm
red hand centers silver shrine, inviting
universal peace with its open palm,
erect fingers like sun rays igniting
every dancing thought and action. Oh, Great
Breather, I clearly see now: when I move
with care, it is you. As one, we create
simple objects of light, streaming our love
in currents of energy, drawing eyes
to our eyes, and our heaven's realized.

WITHIN

Feeling streaming through one word when I pray.

Thoughts trickling among letters of this word,

their droplets clinging to each symbol's day

of reckoning like blood on thorns, absurd

beads of despair sometimes. Sometimes visions

of eternal ocean purifying

all. Most times simple jewels, admissions

of weakness, need and anxious hope lying

on *h* and *l*'s letterpeaks, glistening

barely in strewn strands along sculpted curves

of *e* and *p*. Can grace be listening

to me truly, sense soaked skin, lightning nerves

flashing through me? Can those four letters form

a sound, saving me within my soul's storm?

WHEN I REFUSE TO PRAY

Always at night when I refuse to pray
my bed becomes a witness stand, scaffold
rising in distant dark, no hope for stay
of execution as psyche's tenfold
chaotic chorus—prosecutor, judge
and jury—chant confused accusations
of crimes carved on my soul. *God holds a grudge*
against me! I cry. Still, recitation
of my offenses flows like volcanic
lava through my room's desperate abyss.
A frail ghost steps forth to touch my frantic
face with icy fingers, leans in to kiss
cracking lips. Refusing a final excuse,
demons drag me to my laughing hangman's noose.

I AM TIRED

of blaming old lovers for my sadness.
Weary as a lost wolf, my sick howling
mute to caring souls I longed to caress
but chased away, my twisted face scowling,
my hooves clawing at air, all blind motion
to eyes gone. What now, prowler of the night?
Stay slouched on dark cliffs above black ocean,
long hoarse wail lying of your morbid plight,
draining artist's essence through self-pity?
Or move toward light, seeing dawn approaching?
Time to decide. What's this inside? Witty
whispers of some bright life now encroaching
on this blight? Some minstrel, imprisoned long
through fear's delight, now sharing hopeful songs?

YOU WHO RISE

before the sun, I sense your deep longing
to drowse. I feel your body rippling through
dwindling dark current toward elusive song
from some mockingbird you cannot see. You
who gaze now at fading Venus's pearl
face through dew-moist window, I glint lightning
dancing around your iris, silent whirl
of inner spirit flashing, frightening
demons who lurk in shadows. What power
is this who summons us toward dawn's renewed
fire, helps our linked cells no longer cower
before that terrorizing unknown? You
who rise in predawn grace laced with layers
of dozing stars, I wear your whispered prayers.

DIVING TO TERROR'S DEPTHS

Most nights I gaze at my psychic mirrors,
pray, then plunge through reflective surfaces,
fearful coatings, to substratum's terror
where my disease lurks in disguised traces
of my day's hiding thoughts, coated false words,
most of all my subtle actions slipping
mixed messages to folks who thought they heard
honesty pouring from me. While gripping
my book's blue cover, I review each hour's
content, shine bright light where I spot decay,
beg to not deny its subtle power
to spread and destroy this faith, nor delay
inspecting its cause. I recall its cure:
spirit's balm bringing peace, even rapture.

HIGHER POWER

When I consider what little control
I muster over my life and each day,
it's simpler to get honest and console
myself of reality—the clear way
I may feel my heart rhythm rise from waltz
to rock as I climb a hill, matched by lungs'
surge—body designed by weaver who plaits
flesh, bone, blood and breath, their rampant cells clung
together with intricate artistry.
My mind wanders; my tongue, too. Lungs and heart
find their own way, as do fellows and free
loved ones despite my fears. We rise and start
our days with prayer, it seems, coping with pain,
joy, work and rest. Pray, sleep, and rise again.

CONTINUUM OF OUR CONSCIOUS CONTACT

I deep breathe. I rise. I whisper request
to pay attention. My closed eyes sense sun.
Through open window, steady breeze: caress
whispers back, promising inspiration,
graces my folded hands. Morning's distant
conversation grows closer: lark, car, calls
of small children from far playground. Instant
insight to our true meaning. *We are all
You*, I say without sound, mute lips forming
word symbols, signaling continuum
of our conscious contact. Face conforming
to body's reflex, I lean toward light. Some
force, gentle as lover's touch, soft surprise
of life, beholds me. I deep breathe. I rise.

ALL LIFE IS A GIFT

My body echoes a silent laughter.
I watch others' soulful eyes in meetings,
await their glancing at my eyes after
ages of inner journeys, my greeting
each new gaze with soft smile, my folded hands
as in prayer lifting slowly to my face,
slight bow of head, returning their stare. Bands
of transparent angels share gentle grace,
dancing among us. I see it in your
smiles, dear fellows. These simple things are true.
I hear them in your honest words. They cure
fear for a while. I sit here next to you,
feel your presence direct my sober days.
We carry the message in many ways.

Afterword

Many Twelve Step recovery meetings begin with a member of the group reading from Chapter 5 of Alcoholics Anonymous, the "Big Book." The chapter, "How it Works," begins, "Rarely have we seen a person fail who has thoroughly followed our path." Roger A.'s *We Who Battle Demons: Sober Sonnets* is a map of his journey—and as always when we share our stories with each other, our own journeys—along that path from hopeless addiction to a life in recovery.

The poems (mostly sonnets) that we see here are powerfully vivid—as poetry must be—and rigorously honest—as sobriety must be. And their arrangement here shows the path to recovery through the Twelve Steps of Alcoholics Anonymous. The poems are also arranged to conform to the way we tell our stories: What it used to be like; what happened; and what it's like now.

The first poems in this book tell stories—"drunkalogs"—like those we all tell, and we all hear, about the unmanageability of our drunken lives. What it used to be like.

"Last Night," "Auto Motives and Loco Motives"

> . . . hurtle over countrysides
> of fleeing bodies, bolting me through glens
> of former peace where now chaos presides

and the song—which you feel you almost know the tune to—called, "Song: Kill Myself All Over Again" remind us of what the last days of our drinking were like. We see the paranoia which we have all felt in "Endgame," and the agonizing regret we are all familiar with in "Weather Vain." We also feel the poet's experience of euphoric recall in "Storm." But then comes the beginning of an understanding of our powerlessness as we drive away even our most tolerant friends in "Rogue Waves" where the poet first uses the word impotent: "Sometimes rippling of our bodies beyond/ small obstacles and openings diffracts into impotent light."

When we read the self-image of the addict in "Disturbed Character"

> . . . Can't they tell I'm
> special, a great mind trying to make sense
> of life? How, though I'm a step above them,
> I struggle to understand and love them?

all of us can say, "Yeah, been there, done that." And the heartbreaking poem "How She Danced," which the book opens with, is the story of his beautiful and talented sister who died of our disease, but whose death is not quite enough to make him (or us) sober.

But then the what happened part of the story, the healing, haltingly begins. In the title poem, "We Who Battle Demons," the poet reminds himself (and us) what we are up against as we start this journey; that the odds are against us, that most people who battle these particular demons, " . . . usually lose. Refuse to listen/ . . .Yet a few of us . . . breathless, beaten, may

one day look for our demons and find " . . . They've vanished, inept/ in facing our yielding to graceful steps."

This is the hope that sets us, and keeps us, on our path. And this is where the what happened part of the story begins. This is the point where those of us with a chance to survive begin our recovery.

Step 1 We admitted we were powerless over alcohol—that our lives had become unmanageable.

In the sonnet called "Sponsor," Roger describes his tentative first step:

> . . . When you clasped
> my hand, your clear eyes glowing as Rigel
> and Sirius gleam, at once I sensed our
> first step in seeking some higher power.

The next poem, "Sowing Circle," uses the familiar idiom of AA meetings, "Al tells Bill, 'I'm powerless.' Bill tells Chad,/ 'I'm crazy." And the sharing continues until it is the poet's time. "I'm powerless," he says, and begins his return to sanity.

Step 2 Came to believe that a power greater than ourselves could restore us to sanity.

Step 3 Made a decision to turn our will and our lives over to the care of God as we understood Him.

In "Prayer" the poet describes how he came to believe in God as he understands Him: the "Great Breather" he calls Him. He asks the Great Breather for help.

But the healing does not go smoothly; there is always the backward pull of what we call "euphoric recall," when we remember, not the shame and unbearable regrets of our drinking/drugging days, but the feeling of comfort and release that these things brought us in the beginning, when we fell in love with them and turned "our will and our lives" over to them. Some of the most achingly vivid poems occur in this place in the sequence.

In "Reflection" and "Darkened Window" the imagery is as sharp and clearly detailed as poetry can be.

> Broadway and Bleeker. Northeast corner. Noon
> Weekday. Striding to a meeting . . .
> . . . Gaze at my reflection
> in McEeries' window. I hear applause . . .

Passing his reflection in the glass, he sees a man wearing a " . . . worn, gray Jimi Hendrix sweatshirt . . . He guzzles down a beer. It's '91. A year ago I'm there.

And in "Darkened Window" he finds himself in ". . . Greenwich Village, 5 or after," and he hears the soprano of "silhouetted ladies . . ." call out from in the bar, "Let's Dance!" He realizes,

> I really craved the old routine: whiskey
> sip flowing to lust to maybe crowing
> naked at dawn . . .

But not this time: " I grabbed my cell phone and called my sponsor."

And in the sonnet called "Suicide Watch" he is back to his old haunts again, walking through Greenwich Village. He stops at McEerie's and again watches his own face in the plate-glass window for a moment before he moves away. Still, he remembers the welcoming voice of Barney the barkeep calling "What'll it be?" In "Those Who Thirst" he sees on TV" . . . teardrops of Budweiser cascading from moist brown bottle after the pour," and he feels the remembered taste ". . . creeping down to my tongue."

I find myself especially drawn back again and again to two of these poems. I think because of their insight into how we were drawn to this way of life in the first place: "Always an Allman Fan" and the "double sonnet" called "Eugene O'Neill." I remember the romantic notions that I had about drinking and drugs when I was young, how I—and many of my friends—equated drinking and drug use with being adult, with having "spirits free," with creativity. How so many of us thought, as the poet here says, that we were going to be " . . . special/a great mind" (or a great musical talent)" . . . trying to make sense of life." In the early days of my own drinking I was sure that I could dance more gracefully with good-natured women and fist fight more impressively with other guys my age. And the number of stories told at meetings about making love sober for the first time are legion. We drank because it gave us freedom. We all know what happened to that freedom, how it turned on us and made us slaves. And how some of us found the undeserved grace to escape.

The word freedom reminds me of something one of my professors once told the class about poetry, about sonnets in particular. He said, "By restricting himself to the sonnet form—fourteen lines of iambic pentameter rhyming (in the

Shakespearean form) abab, cdcd, efef, gg—the poet gives himself a tremendous freedom."

In these sonnets Roger A. has brought his very considerable poetic talent and skill to this form, and his poems remind us of the tremendous freedom from addiction we have discovered by living our lives according to the discipline found in the form of the Twelve Steps of Alcoholics Anonymous.

Step 4 Made a searching and fearless moral inventory of ourselves.

Step 5 Admitted to God, to ourselves, and to another human being the exact nature of our wrongs.

"Fourth Step" is another one I keep coming back to. The insight that since drinking had always been a way of celebrating and that after he had finally made himself write his Step Four, call his sponsor and schedule a time to do Step Five, he felt like he should have a drink—to celebrate.

"Truth Within a Soft Flame" evokes a warm memory, creates a vivid scene of a man reading his fourth step to his sponsor. The sponsor nods and says (as they so often do) "I did the same thing."

Step 6 Were entirely ready to have God remove all these defects of character.

Step 7 Humbly asked him to remove our shortcomings.

In the "Big Book" the suggested prayer for these two steps is "My creator, I am now willing that you should have all of me, good and bad. I pray that you now remove from me every single defect of character which stands in the way of my usefulness to you and my fellows. Grant me strength, as I go out from here, to do your bidding."

The prayer in "How Masks Stay Sealed" is, "Keep me on course/ through this day and night. Sober actions, please."

Step 8 Made a list of all persons we had harmed, and became willing to make amends to them all.

In "Soon I'll Approach Them," the poet refers to "The infernal list I dreaded so long." He plans to approach them "softly." He is willing to make amends.

Step 9 Made direct amends to such people wherever possible, except when to do so would injure them or others.

In "To Love as Never Before" he recounts the trepidation we all feel before making an amend: "I reviewed exact words with my sponsor,/then went and knocked on her door." What a familiar story this is! But "She took it better than I had hoped."

Surprising how often it happens this way, isn't it?

At about this point the poems begin to move into the what it's like now phase. People in recovery, as we know, are pretty big on laughing too; our stories are not all haunting drunkalogs filled with regret—although often we even laugh together at these. A friend of mine told me that he was in the elevator of the Arlington Hotel once in Hot Springs when an AA conference was in progress. Two middle-aged women got on the elevator he was on, and one of them asked the other, "Who are these people holding this conference?" "I don't know," answered her companion, "but I stood outside the door of one of the rooms where they were meeting and heard the speaker tell the saddest story. But everyone in the audience laughed like it was the funniest thing they'd ever heard!"

So no one will be surprised that some of these sobriety sonnets are funny; three of them are even jokes—very corny jokes. "Guy Walks into a Bar" is a take on the warning that all our sponsors have given us about "slips": "It's the first drink that gets you drunk," but "Horse Walks into a Bar," and "Valentine Card Walks into a Bar" are just delightful groaners.

Step 10 Continued to take a personal inventory and when we were wrong promptly admitted it.

In "Diving to Terror's Depths" the poet describes his daily inventory,

> . . . While gripping
> my blue book's cover, I review each hour's
> content, shine bright light where I spot decay,

Step 11 Sought through prayer and meditation to improve our conscious contact with God as we understood Him, praying only for His will for us and the power to carry that out.

"Higher Power" and "Continuum of our Conscious Contact" are both about prayer, about an increased awareness that makes us sensitive to the wholeness of creation and our place in it: conscious contact with God as we (are coming to) understand Him.

Step 12 Having had a spiritual awakening as the result of these steps, we tried to carry this message to alcoholics, and to practice these principles in all our affairs.

"All Life is a Gift" shows what it is sometimes like to "carry this message."

> . . . I sit here next to you,
> feel your presence direct my sober days.
> We carry the message in many ways."

A powerful but calming ending; a clear and satisfying image of what it's like now.

I appreciate these skillfully wrought, painfully honest poems. You will too. If you are on your own recovery journey, you will treasure them like the companionship of a good friend. If you love someone who is on this journey—or you wish they were—these sonnets will provide you with a window into their soul. If your life has not been scarred by addiction (congratulations!) but you enjoy reading a poet who is a master of his craft, Roger A.'s *We Who Battle Demons: Sober Sonnets* will provide real pleasure and much insight for you too.

Huey C.